Animal Tales

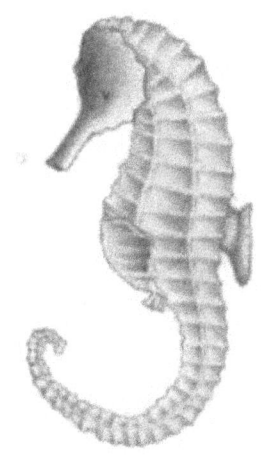

Animal Tales

Poetry for Children

&

The Child at Heart

By; Shelley A. Cephas

Shoestring Book Publishing

Animal Tales

Paperback

ISBN: 978-1-61704-171-6

Published by; Shoestring Book Publishing.

Copyright 2013
By, Shelley A. Cephas
All rights reserved.
Printed in the United States
of America.

No part of this book may be reproduced, stored in a retrieval system, or transmitted in any form, electronic, mechanical; or by other means whatsoever, without written permission from the author. Except for the case of brief quotations within reviews and critical articles.

Layout and design by Shoestring Book Publishing

For information address;
shoestringpublishing4u@gmail.com

To Koji with love

Contents

Preface x

Acknowledgement xi

In the Garden 1

The Bumbler 3

Bobo the Bumble Bee 4

Sweet Butterfly 6

Pond & Water Creatures 7

Lonesome Froggy 9

Charming 10

Froggie's Upset Tummy 11

Timmy's Last Good-bye 12

tale of little frog 13

Hop... Pop 14

A Fishes Lot 15

A Dainty Creature is the Sea Horse 16

Toby the Turtle 17

A Penguin's Day 18

Birds, Birds, Birds 19

Crested Songbird 21

Mal the Mallard 22

Night Owl 24

Dens, Fields & Forest 25

Barney the Beaver 27

Aardi the Aardvark 28

Jonasy Begins His Day 30

Jonasy's Lesson 32

Rules at Play 33

Jonasy's Little Adventure 34

Jonasy's Day 36

Sophie the Seal 37

Sophie's Mistake 38

Sophie's Play Day 39

Bonnie Bunny 40

Bunny at Play 41

Till Day is Done 42

Bright Eyes 43

In Search of Treats 44

Garden Feast 45

Yearling 46

Tuppy's Day in the Snow 47

Monkey Shine 48

Pets 49

Here Kitty, Kitty 51

Ball of Yarn 52

My Pup 54

Author Biography 55

Illustrations Index 56

Preface

This book entails poetry written for children and the child at heart. I fondly remember my mom reading to me as a child. From that time on I have always loved children's poetry. I remember being enthralled for what seemed like hours as she read <u>Mother Goose Nursery Rhymes</u> and <u>A Child's Garden of Verses</u>. When I wrote these poems, I was imagining future mothers reading them to their children. Even as I wrote these poems and this book, I was enjoying them as I remember enjoying poetry as a child. I sincerely hope you will enjoy them, too.

Acknowledgement

Many thanks to Alison for bringing my first book to fruition.

In the Garden

The Bumbler

Bobo the bumbling bumble bee
loves luscious nectar, can't you see?
From lovely flowers, he won't flee
in his garden, full bloom,
as sunshine's shower is the key
to unlock sweet perfume.

We hear his buzzing here and there.
You cannot miss it anywhere.
His buzzes carry through thin air
on a hot summer day;
its beauty that is oh so fair,
he will not fly away.

Bobo the Bumble Bee

Bobo the bumbling bumbler,
a burly bumble bee,
and he is quite the fumbler
of any bee you see.

Buzzing busily each day
in the bright morning sun,
from this place he will not stray
his work has just begun.

He flies from each sweet blossom
to taste the nectar there,
before the hummingbirds come
and take him unaware.

Black and yellow, he's so plump
and furry as can be,
at times you will see him bump
a petal or two or three.

He pollinates the flowers
within his garden lair,
working through daylight hours
gathering daily fare.

Sweet Butterfly

O dainty little butterfly
in gardens you shall flit and fly,
beneath the sun and bright blue sky
your watchers quietly nearby
see magic as you flutter by.

It seems to me that you are shy
and then I ask and wonder "why?"
You're always happy, never cry;
forever seek a world on high,
you never tire or say goodbye.

With beauty that will make us sigh,
well hidden so we're sure to spy
the graceful flights within you lie,
this joy you give in great supply
that we who see you won't deny.

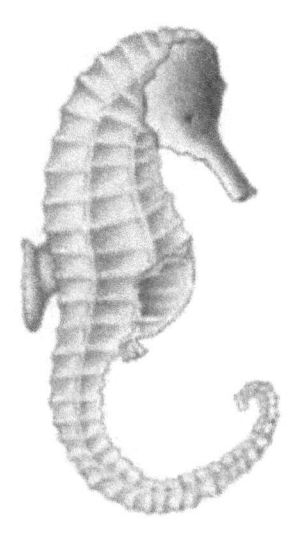

Pond & Water Creatures

Lonesome Froggy

See this little froggy,
light green, he likes to hop and play.
If only he could find a friend nearby,
out in the sunshine where it's hot and dry;
then it would become a fine day
in grass that's not soggy.

But he's all alone, croaking out his sigh
as blue sky begins to turn gray;
suddenly it's foggy
which makes him feel groggy.
So, he begins to make his way
to lily pond beneath a darkened sky.

Charming

Cherished for his sweetness,
charmed as a little frog;
croaks with loving rapture,
crowned in his homeland bog.
Chastened by evil spell
chanted through wizardry;
courtly he'll kiss and tell.

Froggie's Upset Tummy

Unable to move,
so bloated and full;
not really satisfied
but no longer feels good.

Feeling as green as
his lime colored skin,
gluttony a punishment
that hits him within.

Holding his stomach
while wishing for relief,
next time no horseflies
that will bring him such grief.

Now sensing danger
indisposed on his back,
with eyes that are heavy
unready for attack.

Next time he'll know when
his snacking should stop,
until then he hopes for
a quick getaway hop.

Timmy's Last Good-bye

Timmy toad
sits on lily pad
sunning self
in a pond—
tongue darts out to catch plump fly
as it passes by.

Tummy filled
he is now at rest
no danger
is in sight—
suddenly, there's a big splash,
Timmy's gone bye-bye.

tale of little frog

with a whip like tongue
little frog waits for next meal--
swish snap slurp... yummy

flies did not sit well
in belly of little frog--
splash... watery grave

here lies little frog
whose lily pad washed away--
he has at last croaked

Hop... Pop

One day by the side of the road,
we heard a loud croak of a toad;
it echoed through the air
seemed to go everywhere,
then heard a big pop— it explode.

A Fishes Lot

Spending each day in the great big blue,
no worries or thoughts, just the tide;
eating and swimming the whole day through,
no cares but the big fish beside.

Safe when we swim with the school of our kind,
watching for dangers so vast;
staying so close we are not left behind
so as not to become a repast.

Traveling the miles in darkness and light,
feast on whatever we find;
look for a place to hide for the night
from big fish and those of their kind.

A Dainty Creature is the Sea Horse

The sea horse, an amazing creature,
of this you can be sure;
a pet fish lovers would feature,
in a fish bowl, dreams to allure.

Dainty and delicate are these fishes,
endangered, protection a must;
so tiny you think they carry wishes,
you'll gift them to someone you trust.

They have tiny snouts and very long tails
that they use in everything they do;
hanging on plants much like a boat sail
as they eat near the whole day through.

They bring such joy these little fishes,
wouldn't you want one, I do!

Toby the Turtle

Toby the great sea turtle
lives in the ocean blue;
there life he finds so fertile,
he has so much to do.

Swimming is part of his life,
he likes to find new friends;
the sea is certainly rife,
upon it he depends.

There he looks for tasty food
so he'll grow big and strong;
scouts out caves for prey pursued,
he knows he can't go wrong.

Although he lives life at sea,
he still comes up for air;
there's no place he'd rather be
as all should be aware.

A Penguin's Day

You see a little penguin
clothed in his evening suit,
filled with curiosity,
it's fun he's in pursuit.

He will sun himself each day
before he takes his swim,
it's then he and his friends will play,
until the sun shall dim.

In the sea he gets his fill
of tiny little fish;
"they have been my favorite dish,"
he calls out with a shrill.

And when the sky starts to turn gray,
as sunshine fades away;
then quickly home he shall return,
to sleep he will not spurn.

Birds, Birds, Birds

Crested Songbird

There is a little birdie
who flies from place to place;
seldom does its feet touch ground
with treetops as home base.

A songbird with a loud voice
that's hardly ever seen,
but when you hear its wee-eep,
you know it's on the scene.

At times it gets excited,
its little crest will rise
for it is quite the hunter,
it soars across the skies.

Mal the Mallard

Mal the mallard,
an inquisitive duck,
he has no fear
and very little luck.

With a day glow green head
and bright orange feet,
he glances at the water,
his favorite treat.

He's a dabbler by nature
it's in water he'll feed,
like a bobber on fishing line,
finds choice niblets indeed.

He loves this boat house
and anything that floats,
but knows he's more beautiful
as he stands there and gloats.

With his yellow beak
he will quack his disdain,
when he is not noticed
he becomes quite a pain.

Seldom will you find him
all alone on a dock,
for he'll soon join his mate
and the rest of his flock.

Night Owl

Piercing eyes so dark
are brilliant orbs at night,
striking, yet so bright,
in darkness, a lightning spark.

On a branch is his perch,
he watches without a sound,
turning head to look around
from its home in a sweet birch.

Then there is reverberation
of a deep and eerie tone,
the "who-who" from its station
tells me that I'm not alone.

Dens,

Fields

&

Forest

Barney the Beaver

Barney the bashful beaver
began to build his home,
but first he must deliver
twigs from woodlands that he combs.

Near waters edge he works and plays
to build a lodge of sticks and mud,
for in this marsh he spends his days
with his mate through rain and flood.

With webbed hind feet and large flat tail,
he swims through water with delight;
it's in sunshine he leaves a trail
of his work that is quite a sight.

Barney is a mighty builder,
his dam is firm and strong,
for in wetlands it's a great pillar
in nature where it belongs.

Aardi the Aardvark

Aardi's a nocturnal creature,
this is his distinctive feature;
he sleeps daylight hours away,
at night is when he starts his day.

Although he doesn't see so well,
his sense of hearing does excel
and when there's danger he will flee,
sometimes he'll run into a tree.

Each night he spends time digging holes,
you'd almost think he is a mole;
but burrowing is his best skill,
so he can move his home at will.

He must find food that he can eat,
termites and insects are his treat;
providing for his young is key,
so he is busy as a bee.

Aardi might seem awkward and slow,
but he can pick up speed and go,
for he has much work to be done,
before the early rising sun.

Jonasy Begins His Day

Jonasy the tiny field mouse,
he went outside to play.
He poked his head out of his house
to see the brand new day.

The summer winds so hot they blew
across the tall dry grass;
but there were dangers that he knew
could be hard to bypass.

But it was such a lovely day
and it called out to him;
he did not want to become prey
and make his mom's day grim.

She warned him of the dangers there,
so careful he would be;
because he was so unaware
of things he couldn't see.

He knew to never play alone
for this was her first rule;
but he liked to be on his own,
forgetting life is cruel.

Then as he was about to leave,
he heard an awful cry;
it's so hard for him to believe
how close he came to die.

His mother sat there watching him
as now she shook her head;
*'what I told you was not a whim,
listen to me instead.'*

Jonasy's Lesson

Jonasy tends not to listen
to what his mom may say,
and this gets him into trouble
for which he'll have to pay.

He is such a stubborn field mouse
who has to have his way;
never seeing coming danger
as he could become prey.

When will he learn he should obey
the lessons he's been taught,
his mom won't always be with him,
he should do what he ought.

Now that his mom has let him go
to do what he thinks right,
when trouble meets him at his door
there'll be no help in sight.

The day will come when he will learn
the error of his ways,
take good advice from his elders
and at last earn their praise.

Rules at Play

A young field mouse named Jonasy
enjoys a bright morning at play;
out in the dale is where he'll be
at sunrise on a warm spring day...
this time in which he feels most free.

Tall green grass like waves of a sea
sways with a breeze in sunlight's ray;
he and his friends will share their glee
but never far from home will stray,
lessons learned from his mom are key.

Jonasy's Little Adventure

Jonasy the mischievous field mouse
finds trouble wherever he goes;
When his mother lets him leave the house,
concern for him constantly grows.

He's curious about all he sees,
no matter the harm that could come;
while this makes his mother ill at ease,
unsure where danger will come from.

Jonasy is fearless in tall grass
where he and his pals like to play;
they don't notice the time that will pass
or how far from home they will stray.

His pals can see that it's getting late,
that now is the time to go home;
but Jonasy wants them all to wait
because there is still time to roam.

But they tell him "No, we can't stay,
we have to be home before dark.
This is a rule we must all obey,"
so toward home his pals now embark.

He watched them all disappear from sight
as he continued with his play;
when all of a sudden it was night,
he must get home without delay.

On his way home, all the sounds he heard
were scary and caused him great fear;
and one thought to him never occurred,
that his mother was always near.

His heart beating fiercely in his chest,
afraid he'd never make it home;
then he heard the voice that he loved best,
say, "Jonasy you're not alone."

"From your adventure, what have you learned?"
his mother now asked Jonasy.
"That with my friends I should have returned,
and that you know what's best for me."

Jonasy's Day

Jonasy, a tiny field mouse,
loves the morning, his time to play
with friends on a bright sunny day
in front of his underground house,
his mom's rule, for him not to stray.

But he was always curious
when he and friends played hide and seek;
leaving his yard as they could sneak,
if caught, mom would be furious
because of their play by a creek.

"Jonasy, where are you going?"
his mother asked from their front yard.
He should have known she'd be on guard,
that what they'd do she'd be knowing,
so told the truth, though it was hard.

"It's time for you to come inside,"
to his friends, "it's time to go home.
You know you're not allowed to roam,
wrongdoing I cannot abide—
and son... you need some time alone."

Sophie the Seal

A little brown seal named Sophie,
speaks with an adorable lisp;
plays with friends by the deep blue sea,
windy days when it's cool and crisp.

Her eyes are like stars that twinkle,
a bashful little seal is she,
with a soft skin that will wrinkle
when snuggling by her mum, you see.

She loves to dive under huge waves
while searching for delicacies,
then to eat morsels that she saves
on barren beaches near the seas.

Too young to feed all on her own,
her mum will stay right by her side,
till the time comes when she's full grown,
into the sea alone she'll slide.

Sophie, a lovely sea creature,
has a voice that's a deep low bark;
at the same time it is demure
and her mum knows it in the dark.

Sophie's Mistake

Sophie the little brown seal
loves the water sparkling bright;
then she found herself alone
with no other seals in sight.

As her fear began to rise,
'where is my mama,' she thought;
she knew she was in danger
for not doing what she ought.

She didn't like it one bit,
how quiet it seemed to get,
when all she wanted to do
was just get her flippers wet.

The rule, never swim alone,
swirled around in her head,
as she wondered what to do
because all she felt was dread.

Then she heard her mama's call
and her heart filled with delight,
as she answered her with glee,
"I won't leave my mama's sight."

Sophie's Play Day

Sophie and her little friends
were curious as could be,
they hoped their fun wouldn't end
in their beautiful blue sea.

They loved to play games all day
and hunt for food that was good;
then around noon they would lay
down to nap as young seals should.

To search for hidden treasure
was their most favorite game;
it gave them so much pleasure
that everything else seemed tame.

Trouble found these little seals
when the rules were not obeyed;
their mamas would hear their squeals
and go to them where they played.

Then their games came to an end,
their mamas scolded them all;
on this thing they could depend,
because they were still so small.

Bonnie Bunny

Little Bonnie Bunny,
she's just as sweet as honey;
tawny in the morning sun,
with her friends has lots of fun.

Springtime starts to blossom,
each one of them plays possum;
hides in wealth of tall green grass,
silent as the others pass.

See them hop to and fro,
darting quickly as they go;
watch their eyes as they twinkle,
twitch their nose, faces wrinkle.

Little Bonnie Bunny,
her nature is so sunny;
always takes time with her friends,
everyday until day ends.

Bunny at Play

Flippity
floppity,
hippity
hoppity,
a little
bunny plays
today in
golden fields
of heather.

Till Day is Done

Billie, a bubbly brown bunny,
she loves the sweet taste of honey;
spends all of her time in the sun,
near her warren, safe underground—
this place is where she can be found.
It's here with her friends she has fun,
young rabbits that hop to and fro,
through fruit gardens, where they all go
to eat and play till day is done.

Bright Eyes

Bright-eyed bunny
loves his honey,
he's so sunny
today.

Hops down a trail,
this cottontail,
through a green dale
to play.

Long floppy ears,
soft sounds he hears
when he appears
each day.

Hippity hop,
flippity flop—
he will not stop,
no way!

In Search of Treats

Little rabbit
has a habit
runs the gambit
in search of sweets.

Rain or sunshine
will not confine
his need to dine
on sweet red beets.

With floppy ears
he has no fears
all sounds he hears,
even bird's tweets.

Till end of day,
nothing shall sway
him from a way
to find his treats.

Garden Feast

A bashful bunny
hides quietly in tall grass—
as scent of honey
wafts throughout zephyrs that pass.

Her pink nose held high
to draw in this scent so sweet—
she makes a soft sigh,
then follows her garden treat.

Hopping to her meal
her long ears flippity flop—
she tries to conceal
sounds of her hippity hop.

Finding a garden
well filled with fruit and flowers—
without a pardon
starts feast that lasts for hours.

Yearling

Speckled fawn so sweetly freckled,
freckled yearling, lightly speckled;
home in woodlands where you shall roam,
roam in nature that is your home.
Keep close to mama when you sleep,
sleep safe in thicket that she'll keep.

Tuppy's Day in the Snow

Tuppy
a little gray woodchuck,
went out to play on a winter's day.
"No matter what," he would always say,
never fearing the weather.

Tuppy
tried not to hibernate
as all of his friends did every year;
so he would pop out and then appear
to play alone in the snow.

Tuppy
trying to fight off sleep
that would suddenly fall upon him;
quickly to his burrow hole he'd skim
to sleep off rest of season.

Monkey Shine

Twin delight—
one, eyes open
one, closed tight;
good companions,
no stage fright.
They love to play
no matter the time of day.

Pets

Here Kitty, Kitty

Sweet little kitty
with eyes so blue,
wrapped in a pouch,
wonders what to do.

Gently listening
for mistress to come,
or better yet—
it might be her mum.

Waiting patiently,
slowly falls asleep,
then in the distance,
footsteps softly creep.

Hush little kitty,
mistress pets your fur,
settled in her arms
you begin to purr.

Ball of Yarn

A brightly colored ball of yarn,
it rolls across the floor;
as kitty tries to do it harm,
a toy she can't ignore.

She chases it across the room
so quickly she has found
to pounce upon it much too soon,
just makes it roll around.

She sits so still and watches it,
not sure what it will do;
then swats at it a little bit
as if she is on cue.

Into the room her mistress walks
and sees her cat at play;
as kitty cautiously now stalks
the yarn where it does lay.

Just as our kitty gets her way,
her mistress takes the ball;
and now that kitty's lost her prey,
she starts to loudly squall.

My Pup

You fall asleep right by my side,
my best friend in the world;
your love for me can't be denied,
right near me you lay curled.

With floppy ears and twinkling eyes,
you light up when I'm near;
though you may be small for your size,
your bark brings about fear.

The joy you give me every day
means very much to me.
There are no words that truly say
the love for me I see.

I do not know what life would be
without you as my pet,
for all my friends and family
know on you my heart is set.

No matter if I'm down and out,
a faithful friend you'll be
for this I know without a doubt
you're always there for me.

Author Biography

Shelley is single, a trained librarian who loves reading, writing and listening to her favorite music. A born again Christian, Shelley was raised in Connecticut. She moved to New York to attend graduate school and upon graduation made Brooklyn her home. She has been writing poetry for many years, rhyming poetry being her favorite form. She is learning the art of Haiku and Tanka poetry writing and also enjoys writing and creating form poetry. She has worked in corporate America for more than fifteen years as a documentation specialist. Presently she works in a university in New York.

Illustrations Index

bee - http://tueko.blogspot.com/2012/03/quick-sketches-of-random-stuff.html

aardvark - http://www.clker.com/clipart-26233.html

angelfish - http://rode-egel.deviantart.com/art/Sketch-Zoo-Angelfish-275490822

dog - http://hederahiberna.deviantart.com/gallery/

bird 1 - http://etc.usf.edu/clipart/keyword/birds

bird 2 - http://chestofbooks.com/food/household/Woman-Encyclopaedia-1/Birds-As-Pets.html#.Ucrnifm1FPc

owl – http://tristan-despero.deviantart.com/art/Great-Horned-Owl-80329624

catfish - http://www.ccgonline.co.uk/acatalog/Catfish_Pictures.html

butterfly http://www.drawcentral.com/2012/03/how-to-draw-butterfly.html

cat - http://heidischwartz.blogspot.com/2010/02/sketch-dump-feline-above-lando.html

frog - https://www.google.com/url?sa=t&rct=j&q=&esrc=s&source=web&cd=1&cad=rja&ved=0CCoQFjAA&url=http%3A%2F%2Fonlinenews.rv.ua

%2Frozvahy%2Fyak-namalyuvaty-zhabu%2F&ei=s-rKUf6fN-y30gGKnYDgAw&usg=AFQjCNGPBLomJ8AHa5RCSC359betWWdYjQ&sig2=IvDAmkYu0JoVNlBIYMDAYg

mouse - http://etc.usf.edu/clipart/12300/12332/field_mouse_12332.htm

seahorse - http://www.freepik.com/free-photo/seahorse-sketch_533292.htm

seal - http://etc.usf.edu/clipart/keyword/callorhinus-ursinus

www.ingramcontent.com/pod-product-compliance
Lightning Source LLC
Chambersburg PA
CBHW072014060426
42446CB00043B/2544